POINTS OF VIEW

Should Students Be Allowed to PROTEST at School?

By Emma Tunney

KidHaven PUBLISHING

Published in 2022 by
KidHaven Publishing, an Imprint of Greenhaven Publishing, LLC
353 3rd Avenue
Suite 255
New York, NY 10010

Designer: Deanna Paternostro
Editor: Caitie McAneney

Photo credits: Cover wavebreakmedia/Shutterstock.com; p. 5 JOHN THYS/Contributor/AFP/Getty Images; p. 7 Noam Galai/Contributor/WireImage/Getty Images; pp. 9, 21 (inset, middle right) Andrew Lichtenstein/Contributor/Corbis News/Getty Images; p. 11 Klaus Vedfelt/DigitalVision/Getty Images; p. 13 Giuseppe Manfra/Moment/Getty Images; p. 15 Floresco Productions/Cultura/Getty Images; p. 17 MARK RALSTON/Contributor/AFP/Getty Images; p. 19 Fertnig/E+/Getty Images; p. 21 (notepad) ESB Professional/Shutterstock.com; p. 21 (markers) Kucher Serhii/Shutterstock.com; p. 21 (photo frame) FARBAI/iStock/Thinkstock; p. 21 (inset, left) Ira L. Black - Corbis/Contributor/Corbis News/Getty Images; p. 21 (insets, middle left and right) NurPhoto/Contributor/NurPhoto/Getty Images.

Library of Congress Cataloging-in-Publication Data

Names: Tunney, Emma, author.
Title: Should students be allowed to protest at school? / Emma Tunney.
Description: New York : KidHaven Publishing, [2022] | Series: Points of view | Includes bibliographical references and index.
Identifiers: LCCN 2020030746 | ISBN 9781534536517 (library binding) | ISBN 9781534536494 (paperback) | ISBN 9781534536500 (set) | ISBN 9781534536524 (ebook)
Subjects: LCSH: Students–Political activity–United States–Juvenile literature. | Student movements–United States–Juvenile literature. | Debates and debating–United States–Juvenile literature. | United States–Politics and government–Juvenile literature.
Classification: LCC LB3610 .T86 2022 | DDC 371.8/1–dc23
LC record available at https://lccn.loc.gov/2020030746

Printed in the United States of America

CONTENTS

Students Raise Their VOICES

Young people care about many issues today. Students may feel strongly about **racism**, safety in schools, **climate change**, or their personal rights. Sometimes students band together to protest, calling for changes in their government or school.

Some people believe students have a right to protest in school. They say it's a basic right that everyone should have. Others believe that schools are for learning—not protesting—and that protests can be harmful. What do you think? It's important to look at both sides of an issue to make an informed, or educated, argument about it.

Know the Facts!

In September 2019, students took part in the Global Climate Strike to call attention to issues involving the **environment**. The mayor of New York City allowed 1.1 million public school students to attend the protests instead of school, if they chose.

Greta Thunberg is a young **activist** from Sweden. She started skipping school to protest climate change. This led to a worldwide movement of young people called Fridays for Future or the School Strike for Climate.

Making CHANGE

Protesting is just one way for people to make changes in their communities. Young people can't vote, so they have to make change in other ways. They may educate friends and family about a cause, **boycott** companies they don't agree with, and write letters to people in government. Some may feel protesting is the best way to make change.

In 2018, a gunman killed 17 people in a high school in Parkland, Florida. After this, many surviving students decided to protest the gun laws in place at that time, which they felt weren't strong enough. They led the March for Our Lives on March 24, 2018.

Know the Facts!

More than 1 million people marched in events around the United States as part of the March for Our Lives, making it the largest youth protest in decades.

During protests, young people can speak up about their cause. Emma Gonzáles, who survived the Parkland school shooting, helped lead the March for Our Lives protest and spoke at the march.

An American RIGHT

Some people believe protesting in schools is a basic American right. They think that just because kids are still in school, that doesn't take away the rights given to them by the U.S. **Constitution**.

The first 10 amendments, or changes, to the U.S. Constitution are called the Bill of Rights. The First Amendment gives people the right to free speech. It also gives citizens the right to gather and the right to tell the government about things that need to be fixed. People argue that these basic rights are part of what makes the United States a **democracy**.

Know the Facts!

The American Civil Liberties Union (ACLU) states, "You do not lose your right to free speech just by walking into school. You have the right to speak out, hand out flyers and **petitions**, and wear expressive clothing in school."

The Bill of Rights gives people the right "peaceably to assemble." Many think that as long as school-based protests are peaceful and lawful, they should be allowed.

Dangers in SCHOOL

Some people believe that protests in school are dangerous, or unsafe, and take away from education. Schools are meant to be places where people learn and are protected, or kept safe. However, protests can keep students from learning and even put students in danger.

Some protests start in a peaceful way but lead to people getting hurt. Sometimes people join in just as an excuse to act badly. Protests might lead students away from school grounds, which isn't safe. Protests might also bring in people who aren't supposed to be at the school.

Know the Facts!

The California Education Code protects free speech unless it is **obscene** or untrue. It's also not protected if it creates an "immediate danger" of causing students to commit unlawful acts.

Some people believe it's up to schools to keep their students safe, above all else. Rules against protesting are sometimes meant to make the school environment comfortable and safe for students.

Say No to CENSORSHIP

Censorship is when authorities, or people in charge, keep others from **expressing** their beliefs and ideas. Often, this is because those ideas go against what authorities think is correct. Censorship goes against the basic American rights of freedom of speech and freedom of the press.

Some people believe that keeping students from protesting is a form of censorship. Many public school systems state that students have the right to express their opinions through protests that don't get in the way of learning. People who support student protests believe that standing in the way of this right is censorship.

Know the Facts!

A 2018 Gallup poll found that 61 percent of U.S. college students believe their school environment keeps them from expressing their views because those views might be **offensive**.

In 1969, the U.S. Supreme Court ruled in *Tinker v. Des Moines* that students have a right to free speech in public schools. The ruling said students don't "shed their constitutional rights to freedom of speech or expression at the schoolhouse gate."

Permission for TROUBLE

Some people believe that allowing protests in schools means allowing students to behave any way they'd like. They think laws protecting student protests give students permission to get into trouble or not take their education seriously.

When *Tinker v. Des Moines* gave public school students the right to free speech, one judge said it would begin an era, or time, of **permissiveness** that would ruin public schools. The judge said that even a quiet, peaceful protest, such as wearing armbands that stand for something, can take students' minds off the real reason for school—education.

Know the Facts!

You have the right to free speech and peaceful protest in a public school. However, private schools have their own rules, laid out in a contract. You have to follow their rules, or you can get in big trouble.

Private schools often have their own set of rules, many of which are meant to keep students from causing trouble.

More Harm Than GOOD

Some schools have policies that keep protests from happening. School officials may **threaten** to put the school on lockdown, or keep everyone inside. Other schools hire police officers to watch students.

Walkouts (in which students leave school in protest) and sit-ins (in which people refuse to leave a place as way of protesting) are both forms of peaceful protest. Some argue that attempts to stop these protests are more harmful than the protests are. Lockdowns can cause students to become trapped if there's a fire or other trouble. Police may arrest students who are only trying to express their views.

Know the Facts!

The ACLU found that schools with police stationed there had 3.5 times more arrests than schools without police. This also put students of color into the criminal system at higher rates.

Young people around America took part in the National School Walkout for gun control on April 20, 2018.

It's the LAW!

In the United States, all children need to attend school. It's the law. If you skip school without an official excuse, it's called truancy. Taking part in a protest at school or a walkout often means that you're missing school. Therefore, some people consider this to be as bad as skipping school for no reason.

Truancy laws are supposed to make it possible for all students to get a good education. Some people believe if students walk out of school in protest, they should be punished, or dealt with, as if they were absent without an official excuse.

Know the Facts!

The U.S. Department of Education reported that, during the 2015–2016 school year, 8 million U.S. students were chronically absent, or regularly missing school.

You can get in trouble for missing school for a protest. However, it's against the law for your school to punish you for that in a worse way than they would for any other truancy charge.

Know Your RIGHTS

Some people argue that allowing students to protest can make other students uncomfortable. If other students feel differently, they may be offended. They may unable to focus on schoolwork. Other people argue that protesting is a basic right. It gives a voice to young people. It allows them to state their concerns and beliefs in a safe space.

Whether you believe in protesting at school or not, it's important to know your rights as a student. Look at the education laws in your country, state, and city. Look at your student handbook. Knowing your rights can help you make a difference!

Know the Facts!

A June 2020 Pew Research poll found that protesters for racial equality were more likely to be young and nonwhite. They were also more likely to live in cities.

Should students be allowed to protest at school?

YES

- Protesting is a First Amendment right.
- Not allowing students to express their opinions is censorship.
- Lockdowns and increased police presence can be more dangerous than the protest itself.
- Since young people can't vote, protesting is their way to voice their concerns.

NO

- Protests can cause harm to students while they're at school, which should be a safe place.
- Protests can take away from schoolwork and keep kids from focusing on their education.
- Protests can give permission to students to get into trouble.
- Students must attend school, so walkouts are just another kind of truancy.

There are arguments on both sides of this issue. It's important to look at all sides before you decide your opinion.

GLOSSARY

activist: Someone who acts strongly in support of or against an issue.

boycott: To join with others in refusing to deal with someone or support a business as a form of protest.

climate change: Change in Earth's weather caused by human activity.

constitution: The basic laws by which a country, state, or group is governed.

democracy: A government elected by the people, directly or indirectly.

environment: The world around us.

express: To make thoughts and feelings known.

obscene: Offensive or disgusting.

offensive: Causing someone to feel hurt, angry, or upset.

permissiveness: An attitude that allows people to do what they want.

petition: A formal request for change; or, to make such a request.

racism: The practice of treating others poorly because they are part of a different race, or group of people who look alike in certain ways.

threaten: To intend or state an intention to cause harm.

For More INFORMATION

WEBSITES

The Bill of Rights
www.ducksters.com/history/us_bill_of_rights.php
Read about the rights given to all U.S. citizens.

School Strike for Climate!
www.natgeokids.com/nz/kids-club/cool-kids/from-you/school-strikes-for-climate/
Learn more about the School Strike for Climate and Greta Thunberg's work as a young activist.

BOOKS

Stanley, Diane. *Resist! Peaceful Acts That Changed Our World*. New York, NY: Holiday House, 2020.

Thunberg, Greta. *No One Is Too Small to Make a Difference*. New York, NY: Penguin Random House, 2019.

Wilson, Janet. *Our Future: How Kids Are Taking Action*. Toronto, ON: Second Story Press, 2019.

Publisher's note to educators and parents: Our editors have carefully reviewed these websites to ensure that they are suitable for students. Many websites change frequently, however, and we cannot guarantee that a site's future contents will continue to meet our high standards of quality and educational value. Be advised that students should be closely supervised whenever they access the Internet.

INDEX

TITLES IN THE SERIES

Is Safety More Important Than Privacy?

Is Technology Becoming Too Smart?

Should Peanuts Be Banned in Schools?

Should Schools Have Dress Codes?

Should Students Be Allowed to Protest at School?

Should the United States Help Other Countries?

POINTS OF VIEW

ISBN: 9781534536494
6-pack ISBN: 9781534536500
9 781534 536494

KidHaven PUBLISHING

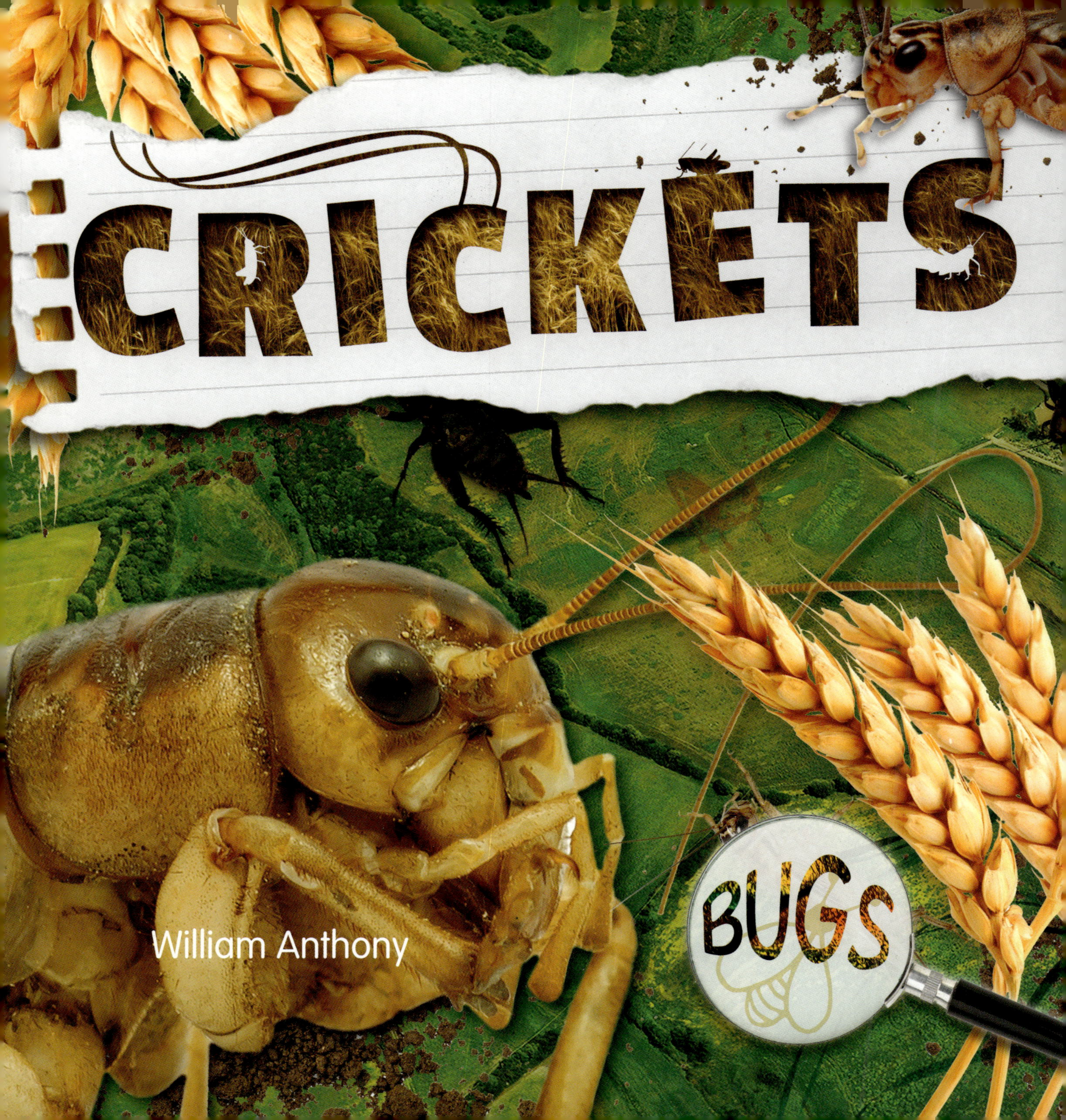
CRICKETS
William Anthony
BUGS